QUINN JACKSON

ADHD Life Hacks

Actionable tips and tricks for women with ADHD to get more out of life

This book was professionally typeset on Reedsy.
Find out more at reedsy.com

Contents

1

Disclaimer

The information in this document is for entertainment and informational purposes only. Every effort has been made to provide up-to-date and accurate information, no warranties of any kind are explicitly stated or implied. Readers understand that the author is not attempting to give legal, professional, or medical advice.

2

Author's Note

I was diagnosed with ADHD at age 24. Thanks to the internet and social media I was able to talk to people with ADHD and realize that I shared a little too much in common for comfort. I didn't think it was possible to get diagnosed with it as an adult but I heard more and more people (particularly women) doing just that. At that time of my life I felt like I was at the end of my rope. Treating the mental health issues I was aware of wasn't doing enough, I was impulsive with my purchases and my food choices leading to a host of issues, and I lived alone. I didn't have any sort of anchor for my life and I couldn't explain why I was struggling. So I found a doctor that would do the test for me (despite having to go into more debt to get it) and I finally had an answer for so many questions in my life. Things I thought were character flaws or moral failings were just presentations of my brain wiring. It wasn't that I just didn't care enough to make my life the way I wanted to, it was that I was experiencing real symptoms of a identifiable disorder.

I am not a medical professional. I don't have an advanced degree in psychology, I never took any college courses in this, nor have I conducted any experiments. What I do have is a Bachelor of Arts in Social Science with a minor in music, a lived experience full of valuable information, and everything I learned in the deep dive I did to learn more about why my brain is the way it is. Not everybody has the time or energy to do the research I did. I sought out experts in the field and listened to their audio books and podcasts and found research on their websites. It took a lot out of me and while I'm grateful I had that energy to put toward it, not everyone does. I wanted to share some of that knowledge here.

I consider myself an amateur ADHD student. While I did go to college, I had three different majors and ended up with a fairly generalized degree. No one particular field felt right, I couldn't picture myself doing something forever like some of my peers. I jumped around learning and doing things to keep my attention so I could finish school and satisfy my family. They were certain my life would be ruined if I didn't have a college degree so they didn't care what I studied as long as I graduated with a diploma.

I remember how exhausted I was the night before graduation. I only had one day off from work to celebrate and then it was right back to my $10/hour job Sunday morning. I cried my eyes out because I couldn't believe I'd made it to the finish line after so long and being so afraid I'd never get there. I didn't know why I felt that way though. I didn't have a name for the invisible force-field that ruled my life, energy, and attention my whole life. I thought I was cursed. I thought maybe it was punishment from the universe for something I did. Until internet memes started talking about symptoms of ADHD and how they manifest in life (as well as incoherent ramblings that sounded an awful lot like my own internal dialogue), I didn't have a lot of hope for my future. Now that I know what I'm up against, and that I'm not alone, I know I can make life work for me.

3

Dismantling Stereotypes

Growing up I didn't hear a lot of unbiased information about ADHD or other related disorders. My grandmother who raised me would sometimes say things about doctors over-diagnosing kids with disorders so they could sell more prescriptions, but it didn't make any sense. Why did we have a name and treatment for these things if they didn't exist? I would wonder aloud if I shared things in common with kids like that and she would shut me down immediately and put me on a pedestal over people "like that". This attitude made me very judgmental about people with any sort of mental health diagnosis, not just ADHD. She made me feel like I was better than them because I didn't need help like that. Like I was a better person for having fewer needs, which is such a silly concept, looking back.

I ended up with a superiority complex that continued until I was seventeen and we found out my younger half-sibling was autistic (we have the same mother). At that point everything I thought I knew came crashing down. I was fiercely defensive of my sibling and eventually I realized that this attitude I had toward people with different needs than me was ill-informed and downright harmful. Once I took down that wall I had built I could finally empathize with people I thought were so different from me. And once you empathize with people who are different from you, you start to realize you're not as different as you thought. And maybe that's what I was afraid of before I knew better. I didn't want my grandmother and my dad to look down on me like they looked down on them.

It's so important to analyze the things we were taught as kids. We might not have been explicitly told "This group of people is inferior to you, you are better than them and they deserve less than you," but we build that narrative out of what we are told and what we see. My grandmother would sneer the R word in reference to people with mental health issues. The disgust and vitriol at the audacity these people had to even exist would drip from her voice. It made me so scared to think I could ever be like them lest she think those things about me.

The only image I had in real life was one kid in my 4th grade class who had ADHD. And I hated him. He was so loud and obnoxious and would interrupt people and he was mean. To me, at the time, ADHD meant that someone wasn't trying hard enough to be polite/well-behaved/successful. This should've raised a flag for me, but at age 9 I had no concept of analyzing things at that level. When I looked at him, I saw who I would've been if my grandmother hadn't trained so many of the ADHD behaviors and symptoms out of me. I saw someone who clearly must lack the will-power to contain these things because they can be contained- look at me, I'm doing it every day! They can't be pushed down forever though, and the exhaustion that comes from forcing yourself to be someone you are not takes its toll on you mentally and physically.

ADHD stands for Attention-deficit/hyperactivity disorder and it now includes what was once diagnosed as ADD. It's a neuro-developmental disorder which means that it affects the brain and how it grows. There are two main types, inattentive and hyperactive, and people can also display a combined type as well. I have ADHD combined type as do most people who are diagnosed. I can't recall learning much if anything about ADHD or ADD in school except that it happened to boys more and it meant you couldn't sit still. That was it. From my discussions with other people I've learned that this level of exposure is not an isolated incident.

ADHD is an executive function disorder. Executive functions are like the core processes that our brains carry out that are at the heart of everything we do. Starting a task, managing our emotions, being self aware, planning and executing, and more fall into this category. There are many ways these can manifest in people with ADHD and they can be different for every person. Some people may also have learned skills to cope with these issues without even realizing it was an ADHD symptom. Many others can still struggle to realize there's an issue at all or that there's a reason for it that's not laziness. They might also feel the invisible pull of a force-field they can't identify, or perhaps are afraid to.

When it comes to getting a diagnosis or any sort of help with ADHD, first an adult or teacher must notice there's a problem and communicate it. I was an incredibly smart child who could do anything with the right amount of praise and encouragement and so I didn't trip anyone's radar for what was considered at the time to only be a "behavioral problem". The symptoms of inattentive ADHD are much quieter than the symptoms of hyperactive ADHD. Inattentive types often experience their symptoms internally with racing thoughts, difficulty concentrating, hyper-associative minds (going down a very long train of thought to connect two things that don't seem similar), and experiencing emotions very deeply. These don't tend to draw too much attention in the classroom or are often explained away as normal childish behaviors.

Hyperactive types experience their symptoms in a more external way. This is where we get the stereotypical image one might think of when they hear ADHD; leg bouncing, finger tapping, shouting out in class, interrupting people when they're talking, not being able to sit still, changing the subject, or sometimes becoming involved in physical confrontations. Between the two types of ADHD, it makes sense that one would draw more attention than the other. The way we socialize boys and girls differently when they're young (for example, valuing nurturing qualities in girls and valuing stoicism in boys) means that they're going to present their symptoms more in line with the way boys or girls are "supposed" to act, as they've been taught. This leads to boys getting attention for their problems more often as they cause classroom disturbance, while girls fly under the radar, sometimes not even knowing they're experiencing symptoms of ADHD.

I was so incredibly well behaved (read: trained), I wouldn't have dared to act on any of the urges I often had to fidget at my desk or call attention to myself in class. I was a good kid who didn't do those things. I knew what was waiting for me at home if I got in trouble at school; a lecture about how ashamed I should be for my behavior. Which doesn't sound as bad as being hit, but I'd do anything to save myself the weight of shame I carried as a kid. I felt like something was constantly wrong with me my entire life and that it was my fault, whatever it was. I was not in a good mental place growing up.

Flying under the radar my entire life made me realize I didn't have a clear picture of who I actually was. I was attempting to hold myself to this neurotypical standard when that was physically impossible for me to achieve. I felt like I couldn't trust the image I had crafted of who I was.

I didn't recognize myself.

Everything I read made perfect sense about this part of the process. The entire first stage after getting diagnosed was about unlearning the guilt and shame and paying more attention to how ADHD affected my life in specific ways. I had to take some time to be gentle with myself and accept that I was on a new path now and things were going to be different.

4

Self-acceptance

There's a lot to come to terms with when we get diagnosed with something like ADHD late in life. It can be really easy to lose yourself in regrets and ruminate over past mistakes that could've been avoided if you knew how your brain worked sooner. The objective is to make peace with what you can't change.

- Forgive yourself for not knowing earlier. You can't go back, you can only do better going forward.
- Accept that you've made mistakes and that the best way to honor those you've hurt with them is to learn how to avoid them in the future.
- Find other people like you, there are vast internet communities of women who have gotten diagnosed with ADHD in their twenties, thirties, forties, and beyond. Try Facebook, Reddit, or other social media sites.
- Seek out professional assistance. Look for a therapist who specializes in ADHD, or an ADHD-focused life coach.
- Learn about ADHD so you can explain it to the people in your life.

They probably don't know much about it and it can go a long way for their understanding if they have an idea of how your brain works.

10

5

Masking and Unmasking

A big part of my particular journey to acceptance was realizing that I had a mask that I put on to disguise my symptoms and appear neurotypical. I was well-trained to not act on my own instincts, but to follow what the normal social rules would dictate and make sure everyone around me was enjoying my company. My grandmother taught me very strict social rules (that were slightly outdated) so my real nature wouldn't cause me further pain. She was terrified that I'd be bullied and I did end up being bullied anyway. Her goal was to make me appear as normal as possible so I wouldn't raise suspicions that something might be wrong with me (or by proxy, I suppose, her and her parenting skills).

What my masking looks like:

- Frequent and fervent apologies
- Over-politeness
- People-pleasing
- Making myself uncomfortable so that others are comfortable

- Putting my needs below other people's wants
- Never expressing dissent in group conversations
- Smiling at everyone all the time
- Not sharing any negative feelings even to people who care
- Never accepting credit for a good idea or a good job
- Higher pitched voice

What my masking feels like:

Exhausting

- Inauthentic
- Unnatural
- Dangerous

When I mask I think things like:

- "Nobody will like me if I don't act like this"
- "The world doesn't like people like me"
- "I need to change who I am to be accepted"
- "I will always be spending this much energy to merely exist"
- "Nobody will ever like the real me"
- "What if I never find out who I really am?"
- "How do people do this all the time?"
- "How much longer can I do this?"

I had been masking my entire life, pretending to be a neurotypical person who had everything figured out. I had an identity crisis when I finally realized what I had been doing because I couldn't parse out what about my personality was absorbed from my mask and what I actually wanted to portray to the world. It was scary at first, I felt like I didn't know myself. So I decided to take the opportunity to figure out what kind of person I wanted to be and start acting like that. I would ask myself if the things I was doing were really fitting with who I was trying to be and naturally I had to change a lot of things. That's the thing about discovering yourself; you have to accept that you might not recognize your life as a result. You can't always keep everything from before and still make progress.

It can take a long time to unmask yourself. I would often say that it felt like my mask was sewn onto me and when I tried to act like I naturally would, it felt just as uncomfortable internally as pulling stitches out. I'm learning that it takes a long time to unmask yourself and it's a little scary. Those fears I had all through my life about people not liking the "real" me but not knowing who the "real" me is were finally coming to the light. There was no going back, I couldn't pretend like that anymore after seeing the pain it brought me. I'd rather people think I'm weird than think I'm a good actor.

One phrase that helps me realize what I actually want to do with myself and my time is "In an ideal world, what would 'xyz' look like?" When I put aside what I think something should look like (a date, a meal, my room, etc.) and focus on my ideal version of it, I can start to think realistically about what I need. A good example of that is a meal. In an ideal world my meals don't require much prep if any, it's tasty and interesting to eat, and I'm satisfied for a few hours so I can focus on other things.

When I entered adulthood I was certain that I was going to cook every single meal I ate because it was cheaper and delicious and I deserved a good meal, like my grandmother taught me. I thought this was how I should be doing things because it was the way I was taught. Holding myself to this standard would often lead me to eat takeout because I didn't have the energy to prepare an entire meal like my grandmother would. Instead of celebrating the win of having fed myself successfully, I would feel immensely guilty that I wasn't living up to her standards for my life. Sometimes other people's standards don't fit with our lives and capabilities. Some people have more energy to spend on certain tasks than others. My priorities in early adulthood were to have a fun time with my friends as much as possible, and spending an hour or so every day making yourself food just didn't fit into that priority.

For a while I still couldn't shake the guilt. It runs deep when the message you've gotten since you were very young was anti-convenience food, pro-home cooking, and anti-perceived laziness. I had to re-frame how I looked at food and fit it into my world. Convenience food exists because there is a need. I happen to have that need. I can't focus too much on what I feed myself because I will be lacking energy for other tasks later if I do. So therefore, to live my best life, I need some convenience foods. And they're still much cheaper than eating out, even if you get frozen meals. Five dollars sounds like a lot when you're buying one frozen burrito bowl, but if you get fast food with five bucks you'll still be hungry in an hour.

It's worth challenging the ideas you have about sticking points in your life. It's not like I sat down and told my grandmother that her philosophy of food didn't fit my life, I let her think whatever she wants to think about how I feed myself. It doesn't have to be a big ordeal, you can just make simple changes to your life that improve your day-to-day. I realized my limiting thoughts about food were actually hurting my ability to feed myself without guilt. Now that I've confronted them, I can feed myself in ways that are satisfying, comforting, and don't zap my energy. It's the best change I've made since my diagnosis.

6

Work Life

Along with accepting the inevitable personal changes that will have to happen, you also might have to reevaluate what your career looks like. Ever since I was young I thought my dream was to be a big executive in an office somewhere wearing gray pencil skirts to work and typing up reports all day. I was taught that this was the epitome of success because I would have a stable career to retire from, regular income, and a sense of purpose.

My grandmother retired from one such accomplished career. She worked for the government for forty years and ended her career to raise me. She has a pension, she found satisfaction in her work, and she's proud of the impact she made in a time when women still got openly treated with disrespect. She told me that I could have the life she did. She said I didn't have to be reliant on anyone to be successful and one day I could retire with a pension and live out my days however I pleased. This was the thing I should want for myself. This was the thing I believed I was capable of for years.

I worked in a bank for almost three years. I thought that I finally found my career that I would retire from and get to spend my retirement just like my grandmother had said. After about a year and a half I started to realize this wasn't how I wanted to spend my time every day. I was barely making enough money to live on and I spent all of the energy I had on masking so I could work with the customers. I didn't have any extra resources to enjoy my life. On top of that, I am not a person who thrives in a corporate world. I asked a lot of questions I would never get an answer for and that created a serious discomfort internally. I needed to know why we were doing things like this, if I didn't know why then it must not be that important. That's how my brain views these things.

I stuck it out for a little while longer and then I had to leave. My next job was in a factory, which started out better, but still wasn't the solution for my restlessness. I wanted to sleep in, I wanted to go to the bathroom at my leisure, I wanted to not have to worry about driving home in the snow or if I could safely get to work at all. I had many friends who had been freelancing for a while and I decided to give it a shot. I'm still looking for the right combination of part-time and gig work to support myself, but I'd rather live a simpler life in the meantime. I've never been happier, even though I've also never been poorer.

Obviously not everyone is able to leave a job just because it didn't work for them. I'm a very lucky and privileged person to be able to leave jobs that didn't work for me, and I acknowledge that. That's not to say that I had an easy time leaving those jobs, but I didn't lose my housing and I always had a meal when I needed it. I was also able to get insurance so I could keep up with my mental health and medications. I had a lot of help from a lot of people during those times and there isn't a day that goes by that I'm not grateful.

7

Working Practically with Your Brain

I had spent a lot of my time working against the natural flow of my brain in all areas of my life. It felt like everywhere I turned I was looking at another failure because I made things harder for myself without realizing. What works for neurotypical people and what works for neurodivergent people are not always the same. There's even variation between other neurodivergent folks too. The up-front work this takes may use a lot of energy, but every little beneficial change you can make for your space is worth the effort.

Take inventory

Sometimes we need to take a closer look at our habits to see where we can improve. It's important to take an evaluation of your living/work space and to notice what influences you to complete a task. This is easier when you take notes as you're doing your normal tasks instead of trying to think of things on the fly.

Learning about your specific obstacles is so important when you have

ADHD because it'll help you ask for what you need from your friends, family, or boss. Start by thinking about these questions and take some notes about anything that comes to mind:

- What in your physical space bothers you the most?
- Are there relationships you would like to improve?
- Where do you struggle to keep things organized?
- Are there tasks you want to get done that you completely forget about?
- Is there anywhere you could physically change your environment to save time and energy?
- What are some things that get done regularly?
- What leads up to those actions happening? Did you put a reminder in your calendar? Did someone remind you? Did you see something that caused you to take action? Could you not physically do anything else until that thing got done?

The biggest change I made after I first got diagnosed is a landing zone for as soon as I get in the door. I used to throw all my stuff on this love seat in my living room and left a pile of shoes next to it that I would try to remember to bring all the way back to my closet. My purse could end up on the love seat under my coat, on the other couch because I just felt like tossing it over there, or even in the bathroom if I really had to go when I got home. This made my already hectic mornings even more chaotic as I would scramble to find my belongings before leaving for work. With only myself to manage, I'm impressed at the amount of chaos I managed to create.

I looked online for some inspiration (thank you, internet!) for ADHD-friendly landing zones so that there's no excuse to walk by the entry and still be wearing shoes, carrying my bag, etc. I made a place to hang my jackets, a place to put my backpack/purse, and visible yet tidy storage for all my shoes. I bought some command hooks for my apartment so I wouldn't damage the walls, I bought some reasonably priced wire shelves for all my shoes, and I set my bag on top. Now I knew exactly where everything I needed to leave the house lived and I saved a lot of time and trouble looking for my things every morning. More time left for me to stop for coffee on the way to work!

These wire shelves worked so well for my shoes that I extended it into my room for my clothes. I hate hanging up clothes, I never do it in a timely fashion and so they just lay about in a "to hang one day" pile adding to the visual clutter of my room. I also hate drawers because I require visual cues to remind myself of things like laundry and if it's all hidden away I won't even notice. ADHD causes a lot of "out of sight, out of mind" moments, and I can't think of any better example than running out of clean underwear because I literally can't see at a glance how much underwear is in the drawer without opening it.

Does my clothing storage solution belong on someone's pinterest board? Nope. It's a little clunky, not particularly pretty, and certainly not minimalist. I think it's also probably not as secure as I'd want for long term clothing storage to be. I'm sure there's a neater and more permanent way to set it up, but it definitely costs more money to do it that way so I'm happy to be patient. I also have a nifty blanket ladder where I hang things that are not quite ready to be washed, but have been worn already, so they don't affect my clean clothes in my cubes. For some people, seeing everything they own at all times might be overwhelming, but for me it's a necessary ongoing reminder system.

Honestly just these two changes made a huge difference in how I felt about myself. I had made an anchor, something that I could look back to and say, "Yes, these things are in their place, I know I can count on that even if I can't count on anything else right now." I didn't expect to feel so excited about some wire cubes and command hooks, but it truly is the little things that make life better. Even more so when you have ADHD.

The Kitchen

I already touched on some ways to edit the way we think about food. As I practiced redirecting my thoughts about food, these are some things I keep playing on repeat in my head regarding food:

- Eating something is better than eating nothing
- Bodies require fuel to function
- If you're too hungry to make dinner, have a snack first
- Food does not have to look nice
- Shredded cheese counts as a snack
- Packaged fruit is just as good as fresh fruit
- There's no shame in frozen meals or takeout

8

Redirecting Your Thoughts

A lot of the work that goes into living a better life is mindset training. People with ADHD can often latch onto a word or phrase and it will play on repeat in their heads. Depending on how we were raised and the messages we were taught to believe about ourselves, these can be positive or negative. For too many of us it's a negative thought we get stuck on and we can spiral downward mentally as a result. You may hear ideas about rewiring our brains or "how to beat those negative thoughts" but our brains need something else to focus on instead. If we just try to get rid of the negative thoughts without a replacement, we're more likely to fall back into old habits and patterns.

It's helpful to look at the ways you instinctively respond to certain things. My family is very judgmental and would look for anything about anyone in public to put them down, most often their weight or clothing choices or anything unconventional about their appearance. I grew to automatically think these things with no conscious effort and it turned out I was an incredibly judgmental person without ever realizing it. I had to start to bring my attention to thoughts I had that made me uncomfortable. Thoughts that made me worried people could read minds and hear how horrible I was being. I decided the kind of person I wanted to be didn't think those kinds of thoughts about strangers. So I took it step by step:

- Bring awareness to your troubling thoughts, either about yourself or people in your environment. Write about what you notice and how it feels and point it out each time it happens, even if it hurts after a while.
- Decide on a neutral phrase you can replace these thoughts with. Instead of, for example, "She shouldn't wear those shorts with thighs that big," edit it to "That person is wearing shorts because it's hot outside."
- Turn your judgments into objective observations and practice all the time. When you look in the mirror and something critical comes to mind, remind yourself of the facts. You are a human with a body that performs processes to keep you alive. Sometimes that means your face is oily or your stomach expands with the volume of consumed food. These are things that happen and they have no moral weight.
- Visual reminders are very helpful, sticky notes on the mirror, an encouraging phone background, setting a reminder on your phone, whatever you need to remind yourself of what you're working on.
- Challenge yourself to find something positive in the people you see. "I like that shirt." "Those shoes are cool." "That piercing is rad."
- Don't punish yourself if it's hard to be positive. Shifting away from negativity to neutrality does the bulk of the benefit for your mindset and if that's as far as you're able to take it, then focus on that as long as necessary. You don't have to try to be positive 24/7, it takes way too much energy and is unrealistic. Bring your attention back to the things you know: You're trying to be better. You will make mistakes.

And you will learn.

We must put forth a certain effort to stop criticizing ourselves. That's not to say that we ignore our mistakes or pretend we're perfect humans, but too often we'll keep beating ourselves up for things we've done years ago. Sometimes we think we owe it to whoever we hurt to keep actively feeling bad about our actions, but this doesn't actually help them or you. These feelings of guilt or shame are not productive, they tear us down little by little and can make us afraid to try to be better people. The best thing you can do for yourself is to learn from your mistakes and actively try to make better choices going forward.

9

Self-Regulation

O ne of the executive functions is emotional self regulation. Most people develop this skill fairly early on in their lives, but for those of us with ADHD we can take a while to figure it out. As an adult I'm now able to look back on my life and realize that many of the times I couldn't explain why my feelings were so strong were because I was having a meltdown. I would get so overwhelmed by a combination of my own racing thoughts, too many external noises, being in an uncomfortable temperature or uncomfortable clothing, experiencing any sort of pain, etc. that I would either become a robot or burst into uncontrollable tears. I've been having moments like that my whole life and I thought I was just broken until I realized there was a name and that it wasn't my fault.

Something that can help folks with sensory overload who have ADHD is stimming, which means to seek out sensory experiences that are particularly pleasant. This is also a tool for autistic people as well. Stimming can look vastly different from person to person. Sometimes repeating a word out loud over and over again can be a stim, flapping your arms, rocking back and forth, tapping a leg, picking at or biting your nails, picking at your skin or hair, and other physical actions that don't require any additional items are common. Nowadays, you don't have to go very far to find items that are made especially for stimming. Fidget cubes, fidget spinners, silicone bubble wrap, kinetic sand, slime, and much more are great ways to seek out a safe sensory experience to counteract the sensory experiences that cause overwhelm.

The reason we want to have options for pleasant stimuli is because sometimes our first action may be self-injurious. Some stims like that include picking at your nails and skin (which can result in bleeding and a risk for infection), and banging your head with your fist or against a wall. These actions may seem silly to people who aren't familiar with a need to stim, but the relief a stim provides can often correct the far bigger issue (overwhelm) to a greater degree than the pain or damage it may physically cause. Stimming is a great tool to use to keep from getting overstimulated as it can give your brain something to focus on even when everything else seems like too much.

People with ADHD have to find the right balance in stimulating activities. For example, my brain felt a sort of comfort and ease (I call it ADHD homeostasis) watching two friends play different video games on two different TVs while I also played a low difficulty game on my phone all at once. I could easily divert my attention to a different game when I felt restless and nobody expected my input on their games so I was free to watch whatever I pleased with no obligations or guilt. I also used to listen to audio books when I worked in a factory and had to do tedious repetitive tasks all day, because my main task was really quite boring. If I only focused on those tasks, I would become so bored that I would want to fall asleep at my station. Some people need complete silence to give their focus to a task, but many folks with ADHD find that they must have another stimulus present to accomplish anything.

Meditating

I feel like every article aimed at ADHD folks mentions meditating. I am cognitively aware of the benefits that come from regular meditation, but unfortunately meditating (which is already a difficult task in itself) is incredibly strenuous for many people with ADHD. Being told to quiet our minds or try not to have thoughts is sometimes a laughable request. Our brains act like hunters, we're always on edge trying to make sure something doesn't kill us while we're caught unaware. This isn't quite as helpful in today's society, but I'm sure back in the time of hunter-gatherers we were incredibly skilled survivalists.

What works better for me than listening to some guided meditation or music is finding something that doesn't require too much careful thought, isn't language based, and requires a set time of focus outside your control. This usually manifests itself as a video game of some sort. I don't like violent games usually, so the ones I end up going for are more like Tetris or my favorite phone game Blockudoku. It's all just shapes and how they fit together for a set time until you lose the game. I've never felt like I was in more of a relaxed state than when I once played Tetris for a few hours without realizing. I felt like I was on a different level of being, there was rhythm to it and comfort and familiarity and I could focus on my breathing while I checked in with my body. And I wasn't bored!

Basically everyone has a different sweet spot when it comes to how much and what type of stimulation they need to feel at ease. Everyone is different, and it can take some experimenting to figure out what works best for you, but it's such a satisfying feeling to find what makes your brain happy.

Mantras

One of the greatest comforts I've had has been adopting several mantras to bring my attention to when I'm feeling off. How well I'm doing and what situation I'm in changes which mantra comes to mind. If I'm having a very low day or feeling bleak, my basic mantra is "I am here. I am safe. I am loved." It reminds me that physically I exist as a person and I exist only in the space I currently occupy. Sometimes our brains can get caught in a loop where something bad happened in our past which can make us feel unsafe even though we are currently fine. And sometimes we struggle to remember that there are people in our lives who care for us. Driving your focus back to these three things is incredibly grounding and is a great reroute if you have well-worn negative paths in your brain like I do.

When I'm feeling overwhelmed or like my perfectionist urge is bubbling up, I remind myself "We can only do what we can do." As humans, we are limited in how much energy we have and how much we are able to handle at one time. I used to think I could do anything if I tried hard enough and the freeing thing to learn is that we actually can't. If we take away those expectations that we need to do and be everything, we can actually focus on the good things we're able to do instead of everything we ran out of time/energy/motivation to do and the guilt that goes with it.

Those two examples are the most concrete times that conjure up specific mantras for me. In a situation where I haven't drawn myself a mantra map to guide me back from my off-topic emotional journey, I count in my head. I don't count my breaths because I lose track of that or I will get too relaxed and fall asleep. I just count to 4 over and over again. I think of it like a measure of music in 4/4; sometimes I picture ballroom dancers in my head, sometimes I am dancing, sometimes it's the random guy on the sidewalk, or even animals. It sounds silly, but choosing something inherently neutral to repeat instead of an emotionally charged word or phrase can often be just as helpful as focusing on a positive one.

The most important part of using mantras is to stop judging yourself for repeating something in your head. Don't berate yourself for getting stuck on something. Negative feelings tend to stick more often because they're just easier to focus on. The idea that we're a flawed person comes with evidence of our past mistakes that we conjure at any moment to feel like we were right about ourselves. It's a self-fulfilling prophecy. And if we can believe that we're still flawed people even in the face of evidence that we're trying, then we can believe we're good people who make mistakes and try to learn from them.

10

References

Attention-Deficit Neuropsychology (ADHD) Part 1 with Dr. Russell Barkley. (2/22/22). *Ologies with Alie Ward.* episode. Retrieved August 5, 2022, from https://www.alieward.com/ologies/adhd.

Attention-Deficit Neuropsychology (ADHD) Part 2 with How to ADHD, Black Girl Lost Keys, Jahla Osborne + more. (3/2/22). *Ologies with Alie Ward.* episode. Retrieved August 5, 2022, from https://www.alieward.com/ologies/adhd2.

DeVor, M. (2022). The worthy project: Learn your value, own it, celebrate it. *Amazon.* Sourcebooks. Retrieved August 5, 2022, from https://www.amazon.com/The-Worthy-Project/dp/B08KWQVF44/ref=sr_1_1?crid=3OCK8RF1U5YRL&keywords=the+worthy+project&qid=1659720441&s=audible&sprefix=the+worthy+project%2Caudible%2C70&sr=1-1.

Nerenberg, J. (2021). Divergent mind: Thriving in a World that Wasn't Designed for You. *Amazon.* HarperOne an imprint of HarperCollins Publishers. Retrieved August 5, 2022, from https://www.amazon.com/

dp/B07TLZSCQD/ref=kinw_myk_ro_title_ab_amzn.

Ratey, J. J., & Hallowell, E. M. (2021). Adhd 2.0: New Science and Essential Strategies for Thriving with Distraction - from Childhood Through Adulthood. *Amazon*. Random House Publishing Group. Retrieved August 5, 2022, from https://www.amazon.com/dp/B08775GG3K/ref=kinw_myk_ro_title_ab_amzn.

Unlisted. (2022, August 2). *Improving the lives of people affected by ADHD*. CHADD. Retrieved August 5, 2022, from https://chadd.org/

11

Conclusion

Sometimes the best life hacks of all are ones that don't involve a miracle product or a strict organization system. Sometimes the most helpful thing you can do for yourself is to forgive yourself for making mistakes and for not being the person you thought you were going to be. Getting my diagnosis in my early twenties made me realize that I had an opportunity to rewrite what my life could look like. It opened a door to allow me to consider asking for and using help from others. It felt like I finally had permission to be imperfect. So even if you just suspect you might have ADHD, let me give you the same permission. If something helps you out, then you now have a better life and you should enjoy it without guilt.

If someone walks away from this book feeling seen, I will have done my job. I might not be on the front lines making neurological discoveries for the field, but I can help people be pragmatic about what they're experiencing. It helps to know there are other people out there whose brains work like yours.

About the Author

While having written scholarly papers in college and numerous blog posts, this is Quinn Jackson's first book. They grew up in Pennsylvania trying a new craft project every two months through childhood and almost constantly performing in a play or talent show. They attended PennWest California back when it was California University of PA and graduated with a Bachelor of Arts in Social Science and a minor in music. Proud cat mom to Stubbs and Roscoe, they have loved reading since they were taught how to at age three. They currently follow their heart writing books, assisting on film projects, and sharing a lovely home with some of their favorite people.